50 THINGS TO KNOW ABOUT THE INTERNATIONAL SPACE STATION

John A. Read

Formac Publishing Company Limited
Halifax

Special thanks to Jessica (Nimon) Swann, former manager of the technical writing team at NASA, for taking on the role of expert consultant on this project. Also thanks to Dr. David Hoskin for his invaluable feedback on early drafts of the book.

Formac Publishing Company Limited and Stellar Publishing recognize the support of the Province of Nova Scotia through the Department of Communities, Culture and Heritage. We are pleased to work in partnership with the Province of Nova Scotia to develop and promote our cultural resources for all Nova Scotians. We acknowledge the support of the Canada Council for the Arts, which last year invested $153 million to bring the arts to Canadians throughout the country. This project has been made possible in part by the Government of Canada.

Cover Design: Tyler Cleroux/John A. Read
Cover photos: NASA/SpaceX/CSA (front), NASA (back)

Library and Archives Canada Cataloguing in Publication

Title: 50 things to know about the International Space Station / John A. Read.
Other titles: Fifty things to know about the International Space Station
Names: Read, John A., author.
Identifiers: Canadiana 20210122706 | ISBN 9781459506688 (hardcover)
Subjects: LCSH: International Space Station—Juvenile literature. | LCSH: Space stations—Juvenile literature. | LCSH: Outer space—Exploration—Juvenile literature. | LCSH: Astronauts—Juvenile literature.
Classification: LCC TL797.15 .R43 2021 | DDC j629.44/2—dc23

Published by:
Formac Publishing
Company Limited
5502 Atlantic Street
Halifax, NS, Canada
B3H 1G4
www.formac.ca

Distributed in
Canada by:
Formac Lorimer Books
5502 Atlantic Street
Halifax, NS, Canada
B3H 1G4

Distributed in the US by:
Lerner Publisher Services
241 1st Ave. N.
Minneapolis, MN, USA
55401
www.lernerbooks.com

Printed and bound in Korea.

TABLE OF CONTENTS

The International Space Station (ISS), is a dream come true for space explorers. A space station expands humanity's reach into the Solar System. It is a permanent human presence in space, and a base for exploration. Humans have been living aboard the ISS continuously for over 20 years.

The ISS is a partnership between five space agencies and 15 nations. It is the most complicated project in history. Researchers from almost every nation have contributed to science on the ISS. Everyone on Earth has benefited, whether it's from better medicine, cleaner water or new technology. We can all thank the ISS for making our lives better and the Universe a lot more interesting.

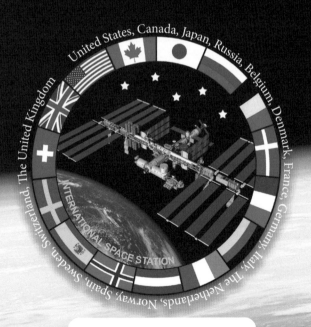

Patch of the ISS showing the flags of member nations

ISS Space Agencies

- NASA (National Aeronautics and Space Administration)
- CSA (Canadian Space Agency)
- ESA (European Space Agency)
- JAXA (Japan Aerospace Exploration Agency)
- Roscosmos (Russian Space Agency)

Researchers have discovered many useful things about human, animal and plant biology. Some of the medical advances from ISS research include cancer-fighting drugs and treatments for Alzheimer's disease.

Advances in physics, chemistry and geology have also been made. These range from the discovery of a new state of matter to cold-burning fire. The ISS allows researchers to study the Earth below, observing natural disasters and monitoring climate change.

Technology built for the ISS helps prepare humanity to explore the Solar System. Astronauts have learned to make tools using 3D printing, grow food, recycle water and so much more.

ISS National Lab

Parts of the ISS are designated a United States National Laboratory. This means businesses can use the ISS to develop products, and teachers can use the space station to inspire kids.

The ISS has been nominated twice for the Nobel Peace Prize!

CHAPTER ONE
A DREAM COME TRUE

Find on page 8

Illustration of Skylab, an American Space Station launched in 1973.

Find on page 8

Salyut 7, the last in the line of secret Soviet space stations.

Find on page 9

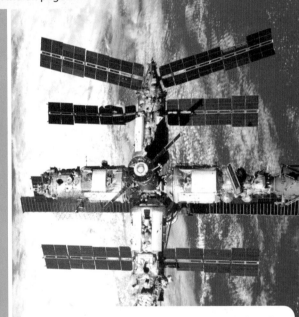

Russian Mir Space Station in 1998, shortly before it reentered Earth's atmosphere over the Pacific Ocean.

Astronauts and Cosmonauts

When this book refers to "astronauts," we're talking about anyone living or working in space. If we're talking about Russian astronauts specifically, we'll refer to them as **cosmonauts**.

1 Space Stations of Our Imagination

Space stations in science fiction often rotate to make gravity using **centripetal force**. So why doesn't the International Space Station (ISS) rotate? The ISS is designed for research in **microgravity**. A rotating space station would defeat the purpose of having the ISS in the first place.

That doesn't mean there will never be rotating space stations. Engineers have dreamed of rotating space stations since the early 1950s. Rotating spaceships may also be used on multi-year missions to the planets. This will help to keep astronauts' bones and muscles healthy and strong.

2001 a space odyssey

A NOVEL BY **ARTHUR C. CLARKE**

BASED ON A SCREENPLAY BY
STANLEY KUBRICK and ARTHUR C CLARKE

What's your favourite fictional space station?

This rotating space station was envisioned by the rocket scientist Wernher von Braun and painted by artist Chesley Bonestell.

If you were asked to design a space station, what would it look like?

If you're a kid reading this book, the International Space Station (ISS) has been around longer than you've been alive! But the ISS wasn't the first space station. The first space station was the Soviet-owned Salyut 1. Salyut 1 was launched to space in 1971. The first American space station, Skylab, was launched in 1973.

Skylab Space Station

Astronaut Alan Bean tests a "maneuvering unit" inside Skylab. Inventions like this were later used by space shuttle astronauts during spacewalks.

Secretive Space Station

Between 1971 and 1986, the **Soviet Union** operated six space stations under a very secretive research program called Salyut.

8

The first "big" space station was named Mir. It was built by the Soviet Union and operated from 1986 to 1998. NASA astronauts visited Mir on the space shuttle 10 times. This cooperation continues today with the partnership between Russia (part of the former Soviet Union) and NASA.

Mir Space Station

Tiangong

The ISS is not the only space station program today. The Chinese Space Agency had two space stations named Tiangong (Heavenly Palace). Tiangong-1 launched in 2011, and Tiangong-2 launched in 2016. Although Tiangong-1 and Tiangong-2 are no longer in orbit, China has a much larger space station planned, with the first **modules** launching in 2021.

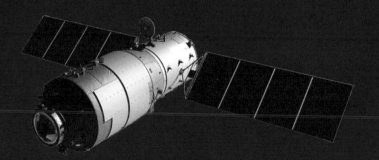

3   Building the ISS

The International Space Station (ISS) is the largest object ever assembled in space. Assembly began with the *Zarya* module, which launched atop a Russian Proton rocket on November 20, 1998. It took 31 more assembly missions before the ISS was complete.

Most of the ISS was brought up in the space shuttle's cargo bay. The shuttle's Canadarm and the ISS's Canadarm2 were used to fix the parts in place. Spacewalking astronauts bolted the structure together and connected the wires and cables.

Space shuttle *Endeavour* on an ISS assembly mission with Canadarm2 and Canadarm.

Launch of a Russian Proton rocket containing *Zvezda*. *Zvezda* is the **command module** for the Russian side of the ISS.

A DREAM COME TRUE

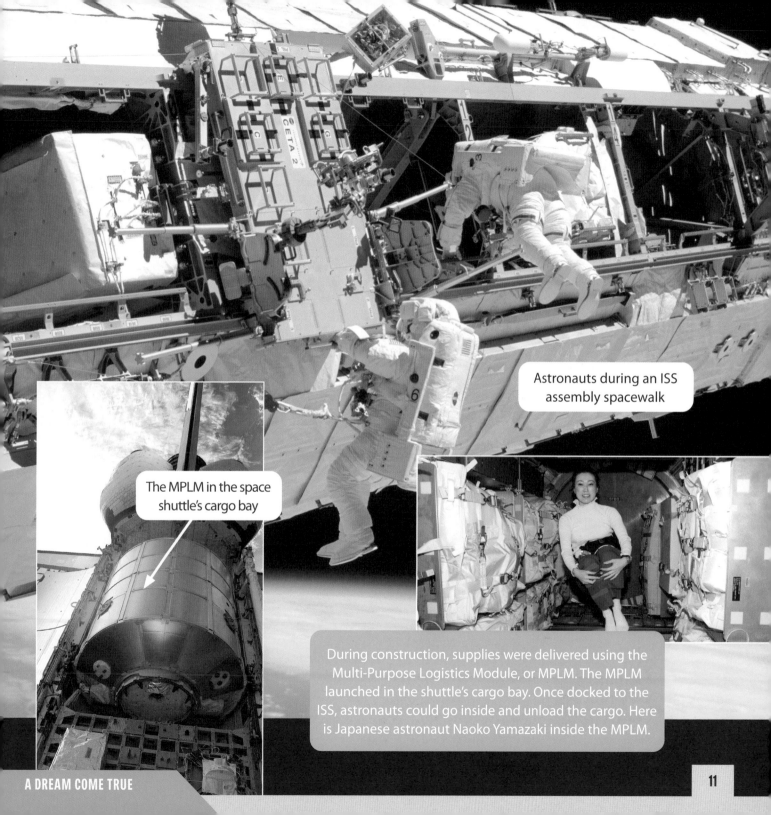

Astronauts during an ISS assembly spacewalk

The MPLM in the space shuttle's cargo bay

During construction, supplies were delivered using the Multi-Purpose Logistics Module, or MPLM. The MPLM launched in the shuttle's cargo bay. Once docked to the ISS, astronauts could go inside and unload the cargo. Here is Japanese astronaut Naoko Yamazaki inside the MPLM.

These white panels are radiators, used to release excess heat from the ISS into space. Radiators are used to cool the batteries as well.

The first thing you notice about the International Space Station (ISS) are these massive solar arrays. Solar arrays use sunlight to provide power and charge the batteries for when the ISS enters the Earth's shadow. These panels rotate on **gimbals** so that they always face the Sun.

The spine of the ISS almost looks like scaffolding. This is called **truss**, and it supports the large solar panels, the radiators and several scientific experiments. It also holds electrical and coolant lines. This truss on the ISS is 108.5 metres long!

The ISS orbits the Earth at over 27,500 kilometres per hour, at an altitude of around 400 kilometres, in a region of space called **Low Earth Orbit** (LEO).

Antennas and dishes provide two-way communication with the Earth, such as voice, video and internet.

A DREAM COME TRUE

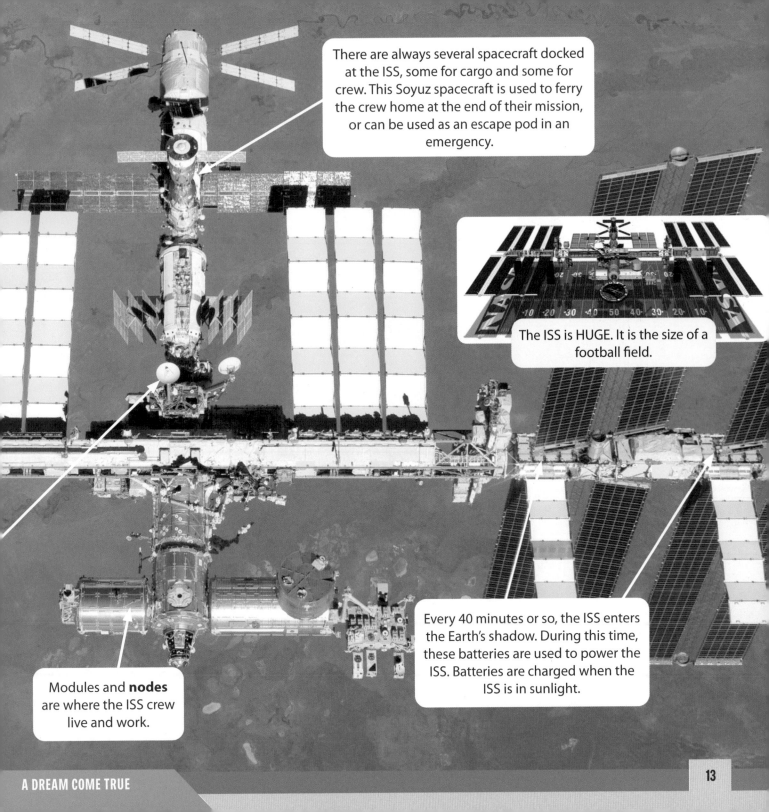

There are always several spacecraft docked at the ISS, some for cargo and some for crew. This Soyuz spacecraft is used to ferry the crew home at the end of their mission, or can be used as an escape pod in an emergency.

The ISS is HUGE. It is the size of a football field.

Modules and **nodes** are where the ISS crew live and work.

Every 40 minutes or so, the ISS enters the Earth's shadow. During this time, these batteries are used to power the ISS. Batteries are charged when the ISS is in sunlight.

CHAPTER TWO
PREPARING TO VISIT THE ISS

Find on page 18

NASA astronaut Tracy Caldwell Dyson is lowered into the Neutral Buoyancy Laboratory (NASA word for pool), to rehearse a spacewalk in preparation for her trip to the International Space Station (ISS).

5   ASCANS

Astronauts typically spend about six months aboard the International Space Station (ISS). Before they go, they must train for several years! The first two years of an astronaut's career are spent in "astronaut candidate" training, during which astronauts are nicknamed "ASCANS."

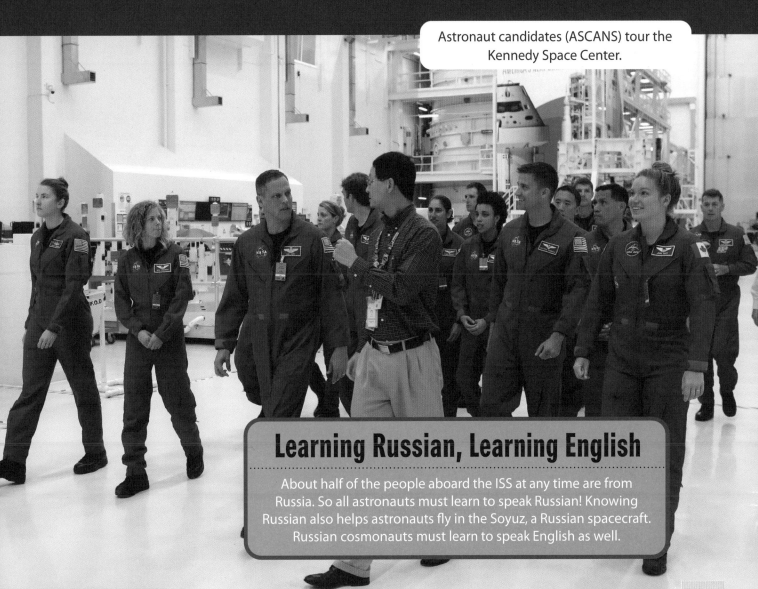

Astronaut candidates (ASCANS) tour the Kennedy Space Center.

Learning Russian, Learning English

About half of the people aboard the ISS at any time are from Russia. So all astronauts must learn to speak Russian! Knowing Russian also helps astronauts fly in the Soyuz, a Russian spacecraft. Russian cosmonauts must learn to speak English as well.

(ISS) includes a visit to Aquarius. Aquarius is an underwater laboratory located off the Florida coast. While astronauts and researchers are working underwater, they are called **aquanauts**!

During their stay at Aquarius, aquanauts test equipment and do experiments. They learn to live in isolation with their crewmates, completing complex tasks using cutting-edge technology.

Researchers and aquanauts working inside Aquarius.

Aquarius laboratory at the bottom of the ocean

NEEMO

Missions to NASA's underwater laboratory are called NEEMO, which stands for NASA Extreme Environment Mission Operations. For more information on NEEMO, visit: www.nasa.gov/neemo

Exploring the ocean floor can help astronauts prepare to explore the surface of the Moon or planets like Mars.

Aquanauts working underwater on a NEEMO mission.

Canadian astronaut David Saint-Jacques holds an underwater jetpack.

When an astronaut uses a spacesuit in space, it's called **extravehicular activity** (EVA), or simply a spacewalk. But how do astronauts train to walk in space?

Astronauts train for spacewalks at the Neutral Buoyancy Laboratory in Houston, Texas. You might call this a pool! This pool has a model of the International Space Station (ISS) that astronauts use to practice spacewalking.

The pool is 62 metres long and 31 metres wide. It contains almost 23 million litres of water, and took over a month to fill!

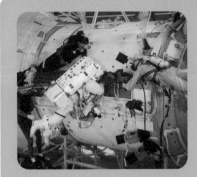

Astronauts and cosmonauts also train in a pool called the **Hydrolab**, located in Russia.

Canadian astronaut Chris Hadfield prepares to train in the pool.

8 Wilderness Survival!

Astronauts train in the wilderness in case their spacecraft lands somewhere unexpected. They learn to make fires, build shelters and navigate. They even learn to find their own food.

Astronauts often train in the Russian wilderness where it is colder than –20° Celsius. They also train in the forests of Maine. This training prepares them to survive in the wild, but it also teaches them teamwork.

Astronaut Jessica Meir completes her wilderness training in Maine.

Astronauts and cosmonauts during a wilderness survival exercise in Russia.

9   Jet Training

You don't need to be a pilot to be an astronaut anymore. However, all astronauts must train in jets. Trainees fly the T-38 Talon, a jet designed for training astronauts. If an astronaut's job does not require them to fly a spaceship, they sit in the back seat while a pilot sits in front.

Canadian astronaut Dr. Jenni Sider-Gibbons in a T-38.

Flying teaches astronauts to think quickly. Astronauts learn navigation, radio communication and much more. Flying a jet also pushes their bodies to their limits. Trainees experience **g forces** of many times Earth's gravity, just like they'll experience during launch. This part of their training is called **spaceflight readiness**.

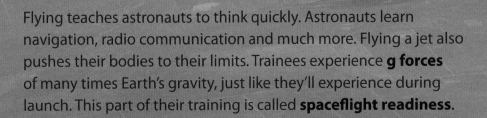

Two NASA T-38 Talon aircraft in formation

Astronauts feel weightless in space, but not because there's no gravity (there is). Actually, they are falling with the spacecraft in an **orbit** around the Earth. In orbit, the "floor" of the spacecraft isn't pushing up on their bodies, so they float.

Astronaut candidates (ASCANS) float in microgravity aboard a KC-135 aircraft during **parabolic flight**.

This KC-135A has just started flying a "parabolic arc." During this time, occupants aboard the aircraft would experience microgravity and feel weightless!

The plane is nicknamed the "vomit comet" because around one in three passengers becomes ill from the experience.

Can you feel weightlessness without going to space? Yes! A plane can be flown so that the floor doesn't push up on you. The plane rises and falls in a path called a parabolic arc. What does this arc look like? Imagine a dolphin jumping out of the water. From the time it leaves the water to the time it reenters, the dolphin feels weightlessness, too!

11 Simulators

Did you know there is a full-size **mockup** of the International Space Station (ISS) here on Earth? Astronauts use it for training and to learn their way around the ISS before they go to space.

During training, astronauts practise with working models of the tools they'll be using in space. These models are called simulators. There are simulators for each type of spaceship, and each tool on the ISS.

Astronauts use simulators to train to fly spacecraft and operate

Japanese astronaut Naoko Yamazaki trains on ISS systems at the Jake Garn Simulation and Training Facility.

Space Vehicle Mockup **Facility** (SVMF)

ZARYA (SUNRISE)

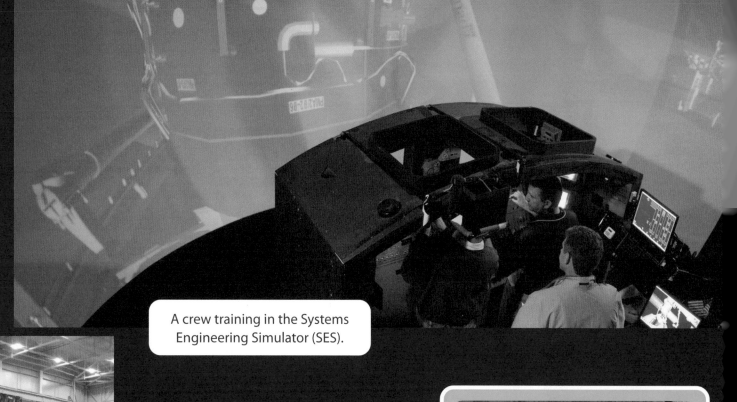

A crew training in the Systems Engineering Simulator (SES).

the Canadarm2. Before each spaceflight, astronauts spend hundreds of hours in simulations.

Much of the ISS training is done in the Systems Engineering Simulator (SES). The SES uses giant screens to simulate what it's like to work in space.

NASA astronaut Suni Williams trains to fly Boeing's CST-100 Starliner spacecraft.

CHAPTER THREE
JOURNEY TO THE ISS

Find on page 26

Astronauts Shannon Walker, Victor Glover, Mike Hopkins and Soichi Noguchi prepare to launch to the International Space Station (ISS) in the SpaceX Dragon 2 spacecraft.

There are a LOT of traditions and rituals that precede a visit to the ISS, especially for those departing on a Russian rocket. Space travellers get blessed by a priest, plant trees, watch special movies and more.

12 Quarantine

Astronauts are quarantined before their spaceflight. This is so they don't bring any dangerous viruses to space.

Astronauts keep working during quarantine. They spend most of their time preparing for the mission. Astronauts also exercise and interview with the media. During quarantine, they can only access certain buildings and a special beach house in Florida.

The beach house at the Kennedy Space Center, Florida.

At NASA, quarantine is known as the "flight crew health stabilization program" or HSP.

A Secret City

Star City was once a secret Soviet city that housed the Soviet Union's cosmonauts. Today, it is a training facility for both astronauts and cosmonauts. Crews departing on the Soyuz spacecraft often spend their quarantine days there.

Astronaut Nick Hague says goodbye to his kids behind protective glass before departing for the ISS.

13 Getting to the ISS

Most astronauts travelled to the International Space Station (ISS) on a space shuttle while it was under construction. During these missions, the ISS was a very busy place. There were as many as 13 people aboard the ISS at one time! The shuttle usually carried seven astronauts: a commander, a pilot and five mission specialists.

From 2012 to 2020, everyone who visited the ISS left Earth in a Russian Soyuz spacecraft. These missions launched from Kazakhstan. The Soyuz can only hold three people.

Space shuttle *Endeavour* docked at the ISS

Soyuz spacecraft launch

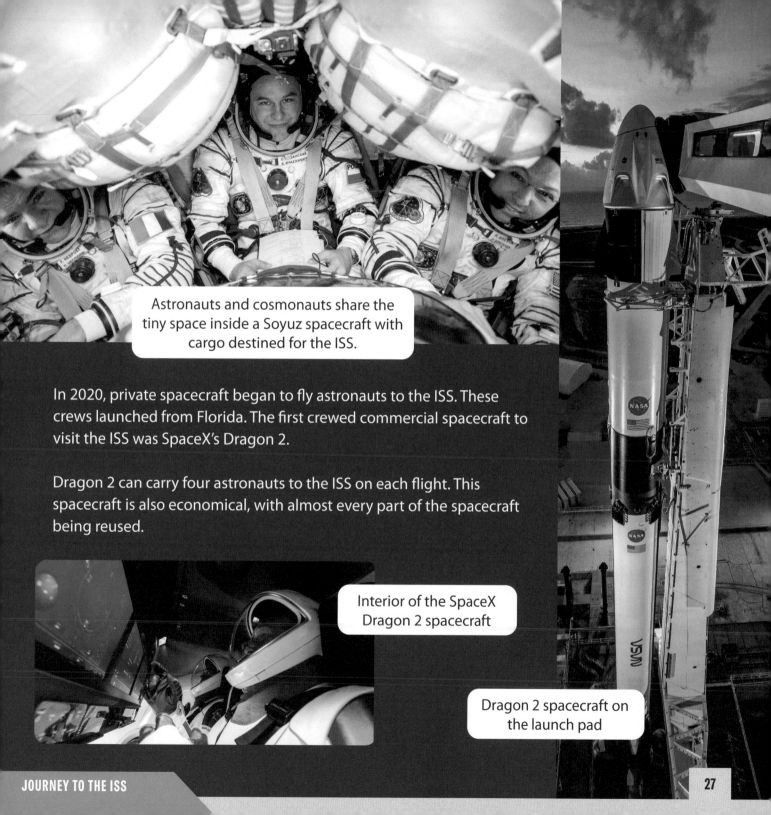

Astronauts and cosmonauts share the tiny space inside a Soyuz spacecraft with cargo destined for the ISS.

In 2020, private spacecraft began to fly astronauts to the ISS. These crews launched from Florida. The first crewed commercial spacecraft to visit the ISS was SpaceX's Dragon 2.

Dragon 2 can carry four astronauts to the ISS on each flight. This spacecraft is also economical, with almost every part of the spacecraft being reused.

Interior of the SpaceX Dragon 2 spacecraft

Dragon 2 spacecraft on the launch pad

The Russian side of the International Space Station (ISS) has two large modules: *Zarya* and *Zvezda* (with a third large module launching in 2021). It also has several smaller segments that act mainly as **docking** ports for visiting spacecraft. *Zarya* was the first piece of the ISS launched into space.

Zarya had its own solar panels, batteries and thrusters. This provided the growing space station with electricity and propulsion. A few weeks after launch, *Zarya* was joined with a US node named *Unity*. As the ISS grew, *Zarya*'s systems were replaced. Now, this module is primarily used for storage.

Zarya means "sunrise" in Russian. *Zarya* was built in Russia, although funded by NASA.

Zarya module before any other modules were attached

A Narrow Hallway

Astronauts Julie Payette (left) and Tammy Jernigan work in *Zarya*. They were part of the ISS assembly team in 1999.

15 Russia: *Zvezda*

Zvezda was launched in 2000. This module has a galley for eating, spaces for sleeping, a toilet and even exercise equipment.

Zvezda is the primary "bridge" of the ISS and contains the "central post." This is where astronauts and cosmonauts meet to solve problems.

From *Zvezda*, the crew can pilot the ISS and remotely control cargo spacecraft. It has several windows, making *Zvezda* a great place to photograph the Earth as it passes below.

Nauka

An additional Russian science laboratory called *Nauka* is planned to be added to the ISS in 2021. *Nauka* will be the largest module on the ISS.

Zvezda module

Cosmonaut Pavel Vinogradov making a video call from inside the *Zvezda* module.

16 The Nodes

Nodes connect larger modules together, sort of like a hallway connects rooms in a house. Each node has up to six ports for connecting modules, airlocks and visiting cargo vehicles. Nodes also provide living spaces, sleep cabins and eating stations!

The first node was called Node 1, or *Unity*. This node connects the **US Orbital Segment** and Russian segments of the International Space Station (ISS).

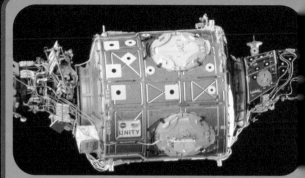

Node 1: *Unity*

In addition to connecting the US and Russian segments, Node 1 also leads to an airlock and **berthing** ports for visiting cargo vehicles.

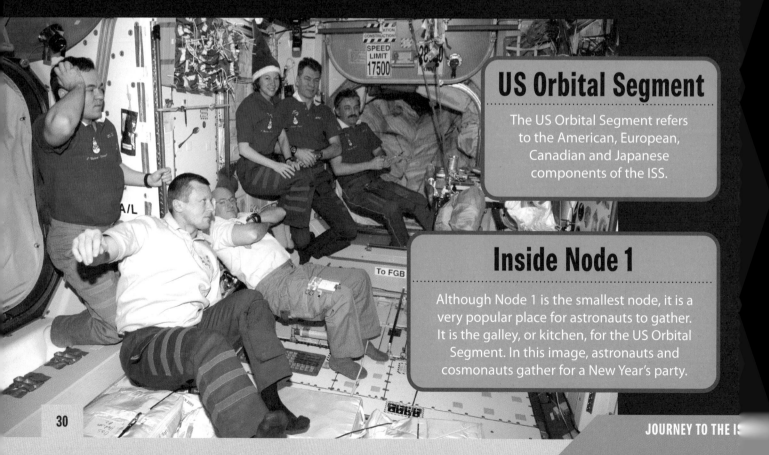

US Orbital Segment

The US Orbital Segment refers to the American, European, Canadian and Japanese components of the ISS.

Inside Node 1

Although Node 1 is the smallest node, it is a very popular place for astronauts to gather. It is the galley, or kitchen, for the US Orbital Segment. In this image, astronauts and cosmonauts gather for a New Year's party.

Node 2: *Harmony*

Node 2 connects the US Lab to the European Lab and the Japanese Lab. It also has two ports for visiting vehicles.

Node 2 has a maintenance station and cabins for four crew. This image shows astronaut Karen Nyberg inside *Harmony*.

Node 3 has a toilet, a treadmill and a simulated weightlifting machine. In this image, astronaut Karen Nyberg uses the advanced resistive exercise device (a bench press machine).

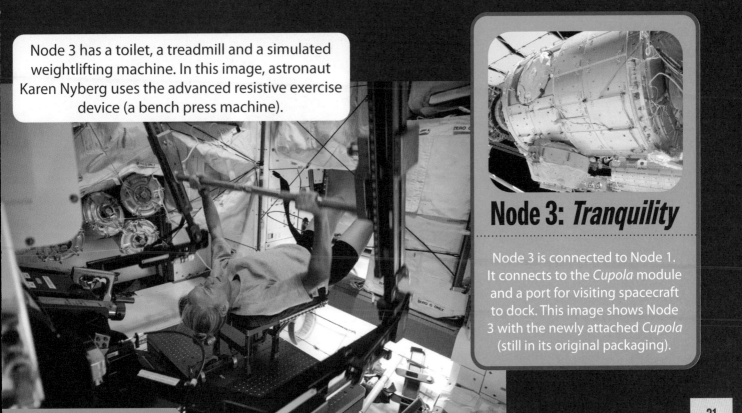

Node 3: *Tranquility*

Node 3 is connected to Node 1. It connects to the *Cupola* module and a port for visiting spacecraft to dock. This image shows Node 3 with the newly attached *Cupola* (still in its original packaging).

17 US: *Destiny*

Destiny module, or the US Lab, is the "bridge" of the US Orbital Segment of the International Space Station (ISS). It was brought up by a space shuttle in 2001. Computers in this module can be used to control most ISS systems, including Canadarm2.

Destiny contains scientific equipment for all types of experiments. There is a freezer for chilling samples and a "**glovebox**" that lets astronauts reach inside a container with built-in gloves. It even has a chamber for studying fire!

Racks

Almost everything on the ISS is organized in racks. Each rack is a standardized size, so experiments can easily be swapped in and out. In this image, Japanese astronaut Akihiko Hoshide installs a rack.

Talking the Talk!

As cool as the official names of the nodes are (*Harmony*, *Tranquility* and *Unity*), astronauts typically don't use them aboard the ISS.

Destiny lifted from space shuttle *Atlantis*'s cargo bay using Canadarm2

18 Europe: *Cupola*

Every crew member has a favourite place to hang out on the ISS. For almost everyone, that place is the *Cupola*! The *Cupola* faces the Earth, providing beautiful views of our home planet and a view of the outside of the ISS.

The *Cupola* was attached in 2010 and has seven windows. The centre window is 80 centimetres wide! The *Cupola* is where crew members take pictures of the Earth and control the Canadarm2. It is also the place to guide visiting spacecraft as they dock.

Astronaut Chris Hadfield taking his breathtaking photographs of Earth.

The *Cupola* and the Canadarm2

Astronaut Stephanie Wilson floats in the *Cupola*, as viewed from Node 3.

19 Europe: *Columbus*

Columbus is the European Space Agency's laboratory. The science onboard *Columbus* is guided by mission controllers in Germany.

Columbus has ten racks, including one called Bio Lab. Bio Lab is home to many plants and small animals. Most experiments in this lab help researchers learn how the human body changes while in space.

Outside of *Columbus*, there is a device for exposing samples to space and an experiment for studying the Sun.

What's "Up" in Space?

Astronauts could work on the floors and ceilings of the ISS. But it is easier if they pretend there is an "up" and "down." That's why there are lights on the "ceiling." Computers and other tools are fixed to the "walls." Having an "up" also means that astronauts don't have to flip around as they work.

Columbus module

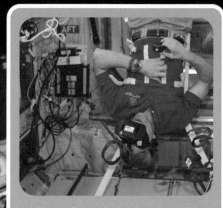

Canadian astronaut David Saint-Jacques participates in a virtual reality experiment in the *Columbus* module.

20 Japan: *Kibo*

The Japanese experiment module (JEM), officially named *Kibo*, is huge! Getting it to space took three space shuttle missions.

Kibo contains 23 racks, its own airlock and its own robotic arm. A smaller module, called the Experiment Logistics Module, or ELM, sits atop the main laboratory and is used for storage. Japanese astronauts are guided by mission controllers in Japan.

Astronaut Koichi Wakata works inside *Kibo*'s airlock.

Japanese Experiment Module Remote Manipulator System (JEMRMS)

Experiment Logistics Module (ELM)

Pressurized Module (PM)

Outside *Kibo* is a platform called the Terrace. It is designed to expose experiments to space. These experiments can be updated or replaced by the Japanese robotic arm, or by spacewalking astronauts.

Space Fact

Kibo means "hope" in Japanese.

21 Airlocks and Hatches

When a spacecraft arrives at the International Space Station (ISS), the crew enter through a hatch. Astronauts going on a spacewalk use an airlock. The ISS has six docking ports, two airlocks for people and two airlocks for supplies.

Airlocks pump air in and out of a chamber. Astronauts going on a spacewalk enter the airlock in their spacesuit, and air is pumped out. When they return, air is pumped in.

Hatches on crewed spacecraft include a docking device that connects to the ISS. There are also hatches between modules for an emergency such as an air leak.

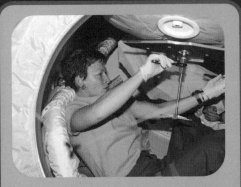

Between the Hatches!

Hatches open to Pressurized Mating Adapters (PMAs) between the spacecraft and the ISS. A PMA is like a jetway leading to a plane. In this image, astronaut Peggy Whitson works in the PMA between the ISS and the space shuttle.

Canadarm2 is used to install the *Quest* airlock to the ISS. *Quest* is the airlock in the US Orbital Segment, while the Russian airlock is in a module called *Pirs*.

Berthing

Some spacecraft "berth" to the ISS instead of dock. In berthing, the Canadarm2 grabs the spacecraft and fits it to a port. The advantage of berthing is that the hatches are wide enough for large pieces of cargo.

The air in a spacesuit is thin, like being at the top of a mountain. Astronauts used to "camp out" in the airlock before a spacewalk to avoid a sickness called the **bends**.

These camp outs have been replaced by a new technique called in-suit light exercise (ISLE). Astronauts spend time in their suits before the spacewalk, breathing pure oxygen and doing light exercises.

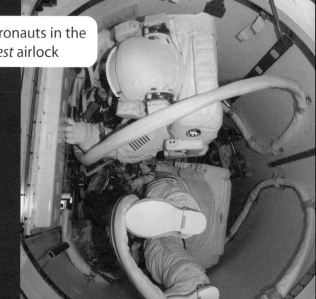

Two astronauts in the *Quest* airlock

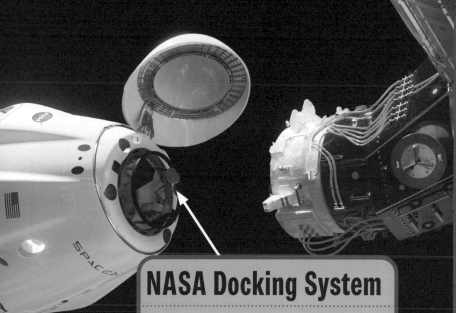

NASA Docking System

Private spacecraft like the SpaceX Dragon 2 and the Boeing Starliner use the NASA Docking System.

Probe and Drogue

Some spacecraft use a docking probe. The probe on the spacecraft connects with a drogue (or cone) on the ISS. Once attached, the probe and drogue open with the hatch so astronauts can pass through.

CHAPTER FOUR
AT HOME IN SPACE

Astronaut Karen Nyberg makes a meal in the "galley" aboard the International Space Station (ISS).

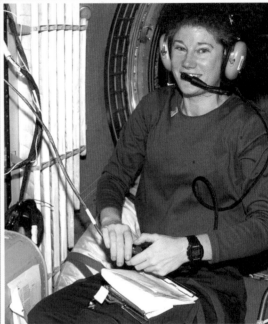

Astronauts use an internet-based telephone system to call their family and friends. The crew also has access to a HAM radio for talking to amateur radio operators anywhere on Earth.

Space Time!

Everyone on the ISS uses Coordinated Universal Time (UTC). What's an astronaut's watch of choice? The Omega Speedmaster, the watch that the Apollo astronauts took with them to the surface of the Moon!

22 Sleeping

There are no beds on the ISS! So how does everyone sleep? Astronauts have special sleeping bags to prevent them from floating away. Crews on long missions also have tiny cabins, just big enough for a sleeping bag, a computer and a few personal belongings. It's a place for each crew member to call their own!

Astronauts try to get eight hours of sleep each day, but it can be hard to sleep on the ISS. It can be noisy, and often cosmic rays strike their eyes, causing a flash in their vision. Their bodies also work differently in space, and they may have to make frequent trips to the space toilet.

Astronaut Cady Coleman in her sleeping quarters.

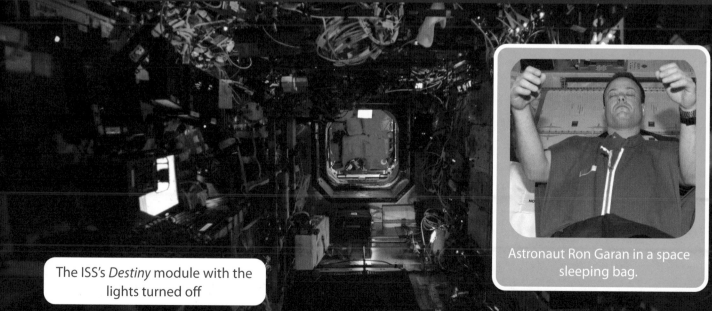

The ISS's *Destiny* module with the lights turned off

Astronaut Ron Garan in a space sleeping bag.

20 Space Clothes

What do the crew wear on the International Space Station (ISS)? Lots of things! The crew have clothes for working and clothes for exercising. They even have clothes for special occasions, like goofy holiday sweaters or jerseys from their favourite sports teams. Sometimes astronauts wear their blue flight suits, but most often they wear comfortable pants and polo shirts.

How do astronauts do laundry in space? They don't! Cleaning clothes takes too much water. When an astronaut's clothes get dirty, they throw them away. The trash goes into a cargo vehicle, which, when full, is released from the ISS and burns up in Earth's atmosphere.

Astronaut Cady Coleman in her workout clothes as she uses "CEVIS," the space station's exercise bike.

Space Pants

If you look closely at these pants, you'll notice they're covered in Velcro strips. This is so astronauts can stick tools and other objects to their pants, so the objects don't float away.

Astronaut Samantha Cristoforetti on Christmas Day, 2014.

24 Taking a Bath

Skylab and some secretive Soviet space stations had showers, but the ISS does not! Showers use far too much water, and put sensitive electronics at risk.

Water behaves quite differently on the ISS than it does here on Earth. It doesn't flow, or pool in a sink. However, thanks to surface tension, astronauts can "stick" the water to their skin, then simply add soap. Once covered in soapy water, they dry off with a towel.

Instead of shampoo, astronauts use special soaps that do not require much rinsing. The astronauts dampen their hair, add the special soap and then dry it with a towel.

Astronaut Cady Coleman washes her hair on the ISS.

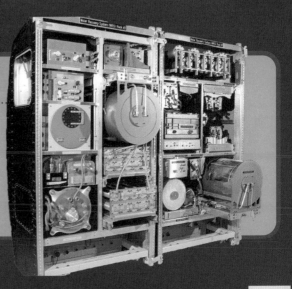

Where Does the ISS Get Its Water?

Originally, most of the water aboard the ISS was brought up by a shuttle or on cargo flights. Now, over 90 per cent of the water is recycled! Wastewater is collected from condensation and urine. It is recycled into drinking water using a device called the Water Recovery System, or WRS. This image shows the WRS before it was launched to the ISS.

Getting ready in the morning is much harder in space. The crew must make sure that bits of hair, fingernails, water and soap don't float away and get caught in sensitive equipment.

Astronauts prepare for their day in a place some call their "hygiene corner." This is where they keep their toothbrushes, fingernail clippers and anything else they need to keep themselves looking good and feeling great. What do astronauts do with their spent toothpaste? They swallow it!

Astronaut Samantha Cristoforetti gives a tour of hygiene corner.

Japanese astronaut Kimiya Yui brushes his teeth in space.

Astronauts cut their fingernails near a return air vent. That way, the fingernails get captured by the filter, which is cleaned with a vacuum.

How many astronauts does it take to cut a crewmate's hair? For some, getting a haircut on the International Space Station (ISS) involves a pair of vacuum-clippers. Sometimes, scissors and combs are used just like in a salon! This often requires several astronauts. One crew member cuts the hair while the other catches it in a vacuum.

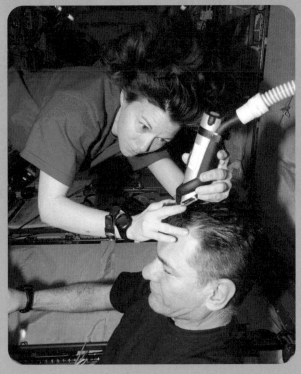

Astronaut Cady Coleman gives astronaut Paolo Nespoli a crew cut.

Cosmonaut Fyodor Yurchikhin cuts astronaut Suni Williams's hair.

26 Space Plumbing

Space toilets have become much nicer in recent years. Astronauts used to use Ziploc bags! But it's still not easy to "go" in space. Urine is collected in a special vacuum tube, with different attachments for men and women.

Going number 2? Astronauts still use a bag, but that bag rests inside the toilet itself. Suction helps guide the poop in the right direction and helps with the smell. Once the job is done, the bag is tied up and pushed into the toilet. When the poop compartment is full, it gets moved to a cargo ship. The cargo ship burns up in Earth's atmosphere like a shooting star — except instead of a meteor, it's poop!

Space washrooms are called Waste and Hygiene Compartments. They are specially designed for both male and female anatomy.

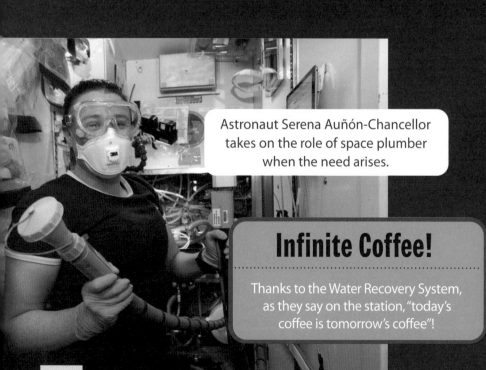

Astronaut Serena Auñón-Chancellor takes on the role of space plumber when the need arises.

Infinite Coffee!

Thanks to the Water Recovery System, as they say on the station, "today's coffee is tomorrow's coffee"!

INTERNATIONAL SPACE STATION

WHC
ACYuK

ORBITAL OUTHOUSE TEAM

In 2020, the International Space Station's bathroom got a huge upgrade. There are now two stalls!

27 Space Music

Music is a huge part of our lives. It's no surprise that astronauts bring their love of music to space. The International Space Station (ISS) has been home to keyboards, guitars, flutes, bongos and even bagpipes!

Music from the ISS has been beamed to Earth at live concerts in Moscow and Germany. In 2019, an astronaut even DJed an event from space, broadcast to a cruise ship! The most famous performance was Chris Hadfield's cover of David Bowie's "Space Oddity," which has been viewed on YouTube over 50 million times!

Instruments must be carefully inspected before they are sent to space. This protects astronauts and ISS systems from chemicals that were used in the instrument's construction.

Astronaut Jessica Meir plays saxophone in the *Cupola*.

Astronaut Chris Hadfield performs "Space Oddity" for a music video.

Astronaut Kjell Lindgren plays bagpipes as a tribute to his friend Victor Hurst, who had passed away.

28 Photography from Space

Astronauts love taking pictures of the Earth. Most of the recent images of Earth have been taken from the *Cupola* module of the International Space Station (ISS). Photographs can also be taken through windows on the US Lab, or the **Russian Orbital Segment**, depending on the angle required for the photo.

Many of the photos are taken for science! The Window Observational Research Facility, or WORF (a popular character from *Star Trek*), uses cameras to monitor the Earth through a large window in the US Lab. One observation was designed to monitor crop growth in the central United States.

So Many Cameras!

A large collection of cameras and lenses fixed to the wall of the Russian Orbital Segment.

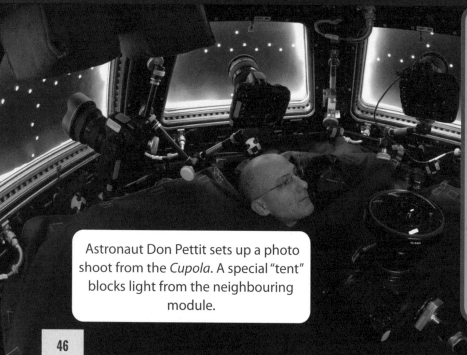

Astronaut Don Pettit sets up a photo shoot from the *Cupola*. A special "tent" blocks light from the neighbouring module.

WORF

Chris Hadfield with an Earth observation experiment (called ISERV) made from a digital camera and a backyard telescope.

29 Space Balls

Astronauts bring their love of Earthly sports to the ISS. ISS crews have fun trying to replicate sports from Earth, or inventing new ones! Baseballs, soccer balls, footballs and basketballs have been to the ISS. Search YouTube for "sports on the ISS" if you want a good laugh. The most popular "sport" on the station is "flying like Superman."

Many astronauts enjoy watching sports, and sometimes get to join in the games. The 2014 Olympic torch was brought to the ISS and even brought on a spacewalk. In 2013, Canadian astronaut Chris Hadfield held a ceremonial faceoff for a Toronto Maple Leafs hockey game.

Astronaut Chris Hadfield "drops" the puck during a ceremonial faceoff for a Toronto Maple Leafs hockey game.

Torch in Space!

In 2013 the Olympic torch was brought to the ISS in advance of the 2014 Winter Olympics in Sochi, Russia. Because of the massive risk caused by open flame on a space station, the torch was never lit while aboard the ISS.

Slam dunk! Bet you didn't know the ISS once had a basketball net! Here's astronaut Frank Culbertson practising his b-ball skills.

CHAPTER FIVE
SPACE EXPERIMENTS

Astronaut Kate Rubins works on a combustion experiment. See page 56 for more information about fire experiments.

30 Virtual Reality

Virtual reality (VR) allows us to interact with a computer-generated world. International Space Station (ISS) crews learn to use equipment with VR before they use it for real. On the ISS, VR is often used to gather data about how humans react to microgravity. But what about fun? Virtual reality games will someday be used to fight boredom on long missions.

Augmented reality (AR) is similar to VR, except the real environment is included. The experience is often called "mixed reality." Crews on the ISS are testing a device called HoloLens, which allows mission controllers to feed data into an astronaut's view as a hologram.

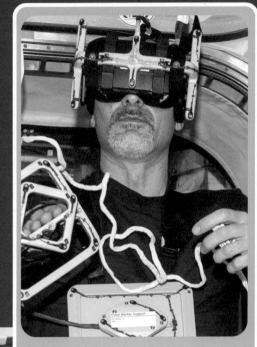

Astronaut Luca Parmitano conducts an investigation using a VR headset. Virtual reality is used on the ISS to help understand the human nervous system and to control robots. In the future astronauts may use VR to conduct medical procedures in space.

Astronaut Scott Kelly tests an AR device called HoloLens, made by Microsoft.

Experiment vs Investigation

An **experiment** is used to test a hypothesis (an idea or prediction), whereas an **investigation** is the process of collecting data.

31   Student Experiments

Did you know that there have been student experiments on the International Space Station (ISS)? These include experiments to study sea stars, bacteria, concrete, space rocks and more! Space agencies often send out requests for student experiments, so keep an eye out for the next opportunity!

Sometimes students work with astronauts by doing an experiment on Earth. For example, when there were ants in space, students kept ants in the classroom. Students were tasked with studying the strategies used by the ants to search an area. Researchers and students are looking to answer this question: Could these same strategies be used by robots conducting a search and rescue operation?

When spiders flew to the ISS in 2011, students across the world set up "control habitats." Students watched videos of the space spiders and compared them to the spiders in their classrooms.

In 2020, the kids' TV channel Nickelodeon sent slime to the ISS. It was a very messy experiment to show kids how slime would behave in space.

Science Project Ideas!

The most important thing about science is that all experiments should be repeatable. Repeating experiments confirms or rejects the results of the original experiment. If you wanted to try these ISS experiments from home, how would you do it?

This experiment, by the United Arab Emirates (UAE), is trying to grow palm tree seeds on the ISS. Researchers hope to create seeds that can grow in harsh environments like the desert.

To find out how you can help with experiments in space, visit: www.nasa.gov/audience/foreducators/stem_on_station

This experiment, called MISSE (for Materials International Space Station Experiment), subjects different materials to outer space to see how they are affected.

Inflatable Spaceships!

This is "BEAM," an experiment to test balloon-like spacecraft. Astronauts are learning how this module fares in space.

32 Astronomy from Space

Since the invention of the telescope, nothing has changed astronomy more than space exploration. There are many telescopes in space, but some of the most exciting astronomy research is done from the International Space Station (ISS).

Our atmosphere blocks most types of light. Putting telescopes in space allows us to see all types of light, including X-rays, gamma rays, microwaves, ultraviolet and infrared.

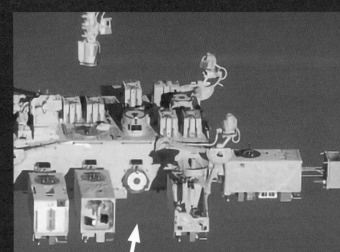

This is MAXI (Monitor of All-sky X-ray). Attached to *Kibo*'s Terrace, MAXI scans the entire sky for x-rays!

These x-rays can be traced to black holes and other powerful astronomical events.

This drawing of a black hole shows the event horizon (the black sphere), disk and jet.

The AMS-02 was brought up by the space shuttle *Endeavour* in 2011.

Astronomy and Astrophysics

Today's astronomers are typically called astrophysicists. Astrophysicists study objects like black holes and stars. Planetary scientists are astronomers, but they are geologists, too. Planetary scientists study planets in our Solar System and around other stars!

The Alpha Magnetic Spectrometer, or AMS-02, is designed to detect antimatter! Antimatter is made of particles like regular matter, but the electric charges are reversed. For example, antimatter protons (called antiprotons) have a negative change, instead of a positive charge like protons have.

When antimatter and regular matter meet, they destroy each other, forming energy in the process, much more energy (per gram) than nuclear power!

33 Plant Pillows

Growing plants in space is called space botany. Astronauts are trying to learn how to grow food in space. Someday, humans may need to grow entire crops in space so that future space stations become self-sufficient. Astronauts would probably enjoy a fresh salad once in a while, too.

Most plants on the International Space Station (ISS) don't have access to sunlight, and require special lights. One garden on the ISS is named "veggie" and has grown cabbage, kale and even flowers. Another garden is called the Advanced Plant Habitat. It is controlled robotically by mission controllers on the ground.

Astronaut Andrew Morgan checks on some mizuna mustard plants. These grow in a plant pillow. Plant pillows contain measured amounts of soil, fertilizer and clay.

Astronaut Kate Rubins investigates the ISS's latest plant habitat crop, radishes!

Dwarf wheat grows inside the Advanced Plant Habitat aboard the ISS.

34 3D Printing

What do you do on your spaceship if something breaks? If you're on the ISS, spare parts arrive each month. But what if you're on your way to Mars? Astronauts must learn to make parts if they are going to explore the Solar System. That's where 3D printing comes in!

A 3D printer uses plastic or metal filament to make parts. It can also make parts for other 3D printers! The first 3D printer was sent to space in 2014. The ISS also has a ReFabricator, which takes old parts and recycles them into filament.

Astronaut Samantha Cristoforetti at the ISS's 3D printer.

This device, called the ReFabricator, recycles old parts, turning them into filament for the 3D printer.

One of the first tools 3D printed in space was this tiny ratchet.

Fire in space is extremely dangerous, so it is important to understand how fire behaves. Burning is quite different in space than on Earth. Even the shape of a flame is different! Studying fire on the International Space Station (ISS) led to the amazing discovery of cool-burning flames. This could lead to more fuel-efficient engines.

In space, warm air does not rise! Instead, flames form a sphere around the fuel. Astronauts study materials to see if they are more flammable in space than on Earth. They also want to know how fires spread in microgravity. These experiments will reduce the risk of fires aboard spacecraft.

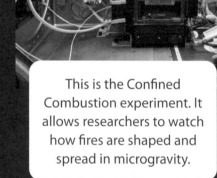

This is the Confined Combustion experiment. It allows researchers to watch how fires are shaped and spread in microgravity.

Astronaut Alexander Gerst with an experiment called BASS (Burning and Suppression of Solids).

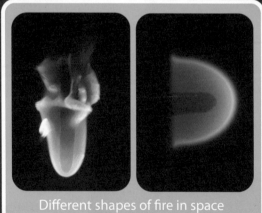

Different shapes of fire in space

36 ISS Aquariums

Can fish live in space? Absolutely! Fish have been flying to space with astronauts since 1973. The ISS's first fish tank, called the Aquatic Habitat or AQH, was added in 2012. The tank's lighting, water chemistry and fish feeding are all handled automatically. Scientists on Earth use video cameras to observe the fish.

Fish mature quickly, so several generations can spawn during a single mission, and scientists can observe how each generation evolves in microgravity. Some fish, like medaka fish, are slightly transparent. This allows researchers to observe how their organs work and how their bones adapt to life in space.

Space Fish

Medaka fish, like these, flew to the ISS and were kept in the AQH. While in space, researchers observed the fish growing from minnows to adults.

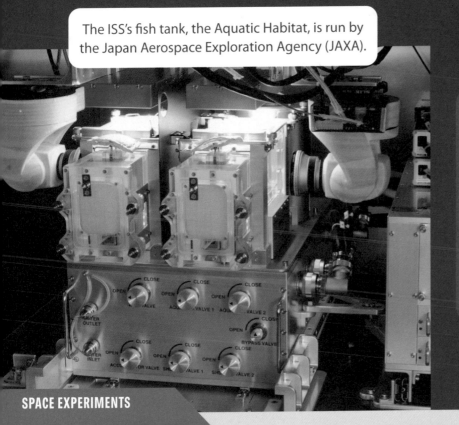

The ISS's fish tank, the Aquatic Habitat, is run by the Japan Aerospace Exploration Agency (JAXA).

Fluid Physics

The water in these tanks is a fluid, and fluids behave much differently in space than they do on Earth. There are fluids in our bodies, fluids in rocket engines and fluids in experiments like these fish tanks. Fluid physics is one of the most important research areas done on the ISS.

37 Animals on the ISS

The International Space Station (ISS) is home to many animals, but not the ones you might think. The days of dogs, cats, monkeys and chimps in space are behind us. Most species that travel to the ISS are small. The largest animal on the ISS is a mouse!

Some of the most important medical discoveries are made with rodents. Mice on the ISS are bred for medical research. Investigators studying these space mice hope to find cures for age-related diseases.

The Ant Forage Habitat Facility is an investigation into how ants search for food in microgravity.

Astronauts Jessica Meir and Andrew Morgan studying mice in the Life Sciences Glovebox (LSG).

Animal Welfare

The US Department of Agriculture's Institutional Animal Care and Use Committee (IACUC) holds NASA to a very high standard. They make sure that all animals are treated humanely.

What types of animals have visited the ISS? Visitors have included fruit flies, houseflies, spiders, worms, squid, ants, sea stars, water fleas, shrimp, beetles and even snails.

Racetracking!

Mice adapt quickly to life in space. They teach themselves to run in circles, using centripetal force to keep them on the walls. This mouse exercise routine has been dubbed "Racetracking."

Extremophiles

A very special animal, called the tardigrade or water bear, is a frequent visitor to the ISS. These microscopic animals, typically found in pond water, can survive extreme temperatures. They can even survive the vacuum of space. It's for this reason they've been called **extremophiles**!

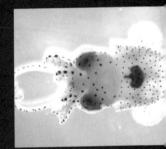

Climate change is the biggest threat facing humanity today. The reality of a changing climate, caused by humans, is easily measured from space.

Outside of the International Space Station (ISS), a device called the Cloud-Aerosol Transport System, or CATS, uses laser-radar (lidar) to study **aerosols**, a type of pollution. The device shoots a laser at the atmosphere to make pollution maps. An instrument called RapidScat used radar to detect moving air. RapidScat monitored hurricanes by measuring wind speeds over the ocean.

Can students use the ISS to study climate change? Yes! Students can request a Crew Earth Observation, or CEO. This is a request for an astronaut to take a picture of an event on Earth, like forest fires or coastal erosion.

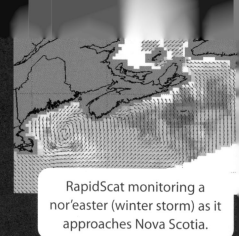

RapidScat monitoring a nor'easter (winter storm) as it approaches Nova Scotia.

Technicians prepare RapidScat for launch.

The CATS (Cloud-Aerosol Transport System) instrument before being launched to the ISS.

Remote Sensing

Remote sensing is a term used to describe scientific observations taken from a distance.

39 Robonaut

The human body is amazing. It can climb, twist, grab, push and haul. These traits have typically been difficult for robots to do as well as a person can. But researchers intend to change that. Robots that move like humans, called humanoid robots, could replace humans performing dangerous tasks.

Meet Robonaut, the first humanoid robot in space. Robonaut has arms and hands that move like a human. That means that Robonaut, in theory, can do what a human does! Robonaut has been on the ISS since 2012, but didn't get legs until 2014. Robonaut hasn't replaced humans, yet. It is a research tool for developing technologies for future robots.

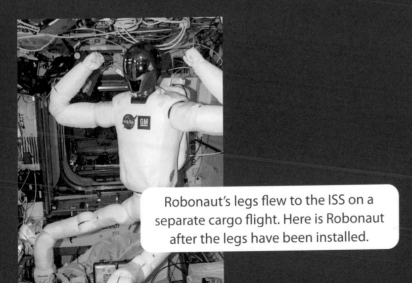

Robonaut's legs flew to the ISS on a separate cargo flight. Here is Robonaut after the legs have been installed.

Someday, humanoid robots could pull people from burning buildings, or fix gas and chemical leaks. In space, they can perform maintenance, or even conduct a spacewalk without human intervention.

CHAPTER SIX
SPACE STATION OPERATIONS

Find Canadarm2 on page 64

Getting Paid

Most astronauts collect a salary from the government, which they receive whether they are in space or not. Russian cosmonauts receive extra money for each day spent in space, as well as bonuses for good performance and docked pay for poor performance. This makes the accounting quite complex!

Astronaut Christina Koch at the *Cupola's* robotics workstation as she prepares to operate Canadarm2.

40 Computer Power!

On Earth, kids and adults spend much of their days using computers, tablets and phones. Life on the International Space Station (ISS) isn't much different. Astronauts also spend much of their time looking at screens.

On the ISS, computers use an **operating system** called Linux to run important systems. Computers for everyday use, such as browsing the internet, use Windows. Astronauts can post to social media, share pictures and chat with the public.

IBM ThinkPad

Most of the computers on the ISS are IBM ThinkPad laptops. In fact, over 50 ThinkPads have been used on the ISS. This image shows astronaut Cady Coleman using an IBM ThinkPad.

Cosmic Rays vs Computers

Cosmic rays are little bits of matter moving at incredible speed. These particles can pass through the walls of the ISS and damage computer hardware. For important ISS operations, there are three computers: a primary, a backup and a standby.

Tablet computers such as iPads are used on the ISS. Here's astronaut Peggy Whitson using an iPad to schedule tasks.

41 Canadarm2

One of the most important tools on the International Space Station (ISS) is a giant robotic arm called Canadarm2. It catches incoming cargo spacecraft and performs maintenance, and was even used to assemble the ISS! Canadarm2 was built by MDA Systems in Ontario, Canada. The first Canadarm was used on space shuttles.

Canadians are so proud of their contribution to the ISS that Canadarm2 and Dextre are featured on the Canadian five-dollar bill!

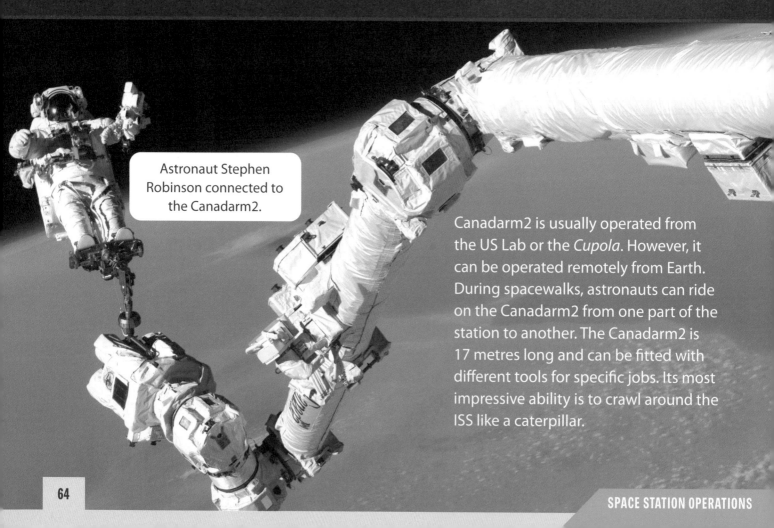

Astronaut Stephen Robinson connected to the Canadarm2.

Canadarm2 is usually operated from the US Lab or the *Cupola*. However, it can be operated remotely from Earth. During spacewalks, astronauts can ride on the Canadarm2 from one part of the station to another. The Canadarm2 is 17 metres long and can be fitted with different tools for specific jobs. Its most impressive ability is to crawl around the ISS like a caterpillar.

Japanese Experiment Module Remote Manipulator System (JEMRMS)

Cosmonaut working with a Strela crane.

Canadarm2 is not the only robotic arm on the ISS. The Japanese Experiment Module Remote Manipulator System (JEMRMS) is a robotic arm attached to *Kibo*. Robotic arms are also not the only "arms" on the station. There are also cranes, called Strela, to move supplies and crew around the Russian Orbital Segment.

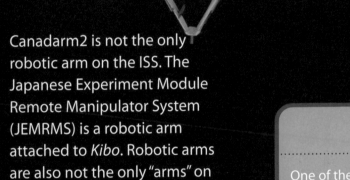

Dextre

One of the tools used on Canadarm2 is a "robotic helper" called the Special Purpose Dexterous Manipulator or simply "Dextre."

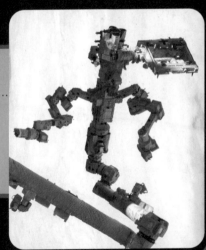

42 Mission Control

The International Space Station (ISS) team on Earth is much more than a few rows of people at computers, looking at giant screens. That room full of people is called Mission Control, and their job is to, well, control the mission!

The flight director is in charge of the room, making sure what needs to get done, gets done. The training team prepares for every worst-case scenario, and the engineering team is ready to solve problems when they arise.

The ISS employs tens of thousands of people from around the world. These are workers from every educational background, including the arts and the sciences. This worldwide team keeps the astronauts busy, healthy and safe.

The Mission Control patch for NASA includes the phrase *"res gesta per excellentiam,"* which means "achieve through excellence."

Mission Control Houston is home to the flight control team (FCT). The FCT is crewed 24 hours a day, every day.

ISS Mission Control
Moscow in Russia

"Montreal"

There is a Mission Control just outside of Montreal, Quebec. This robotics centre supports Canadarm2.

The ISS can be piloted by the astronauts, or by mission controllers in the United States or Russia. The ISS can be steered using a set of gyroscopes called Control Moment Gyros! By twisting these massive spinning wheels, the entire space station will turn! The ISS turns to keep its solar panels pointed at the Sun, and its radio equipment pointed at Earth.

A worker inspects a new Control Moment Gyro before it launches to the ISS.

A spacewalk, or extravehicular activity (EVA), is often the highlight of an astronaut's career. While floating above the Earth in their spacesuit, they witness a breathtaking view. Training for a spacewalk happens months in advance, with each task carefully planned.

Spacewalks happen for many reasons. They are mainly done to replace systems or install experiments. It takes a whole team of people on Earth to support spacewalking astronauts. Astronauts inside the International Space Station (ISS) also assist the spacewalkers. They use Canadarm2 and work through checklists along with their teammates outside.

Russian Spacesuits

Russian spacesuits, known as Orlan suits, are very different from NASA's spacesuits. Cosmonauts wear blue liquid cooling garments, and enter their suits through a door in the back.

Astronaut Nicholas Patrick on a spacewalk during ISS construction.

The Spacesuit
Extravehicular Mobility Unit (EMU)

The helmet contains a sun visor and can be fitted with lights and video cameras.

The spacesuit contains a drink bag so that astronauts can access water via a tube in their helmet.

The control module allows the astronaut to control the pressure and temperature of the suit, as well as operate their radio.

On their wrist, astronauts wear a checklist detailing their tasks, as well as a mirror for reading the controls on their chest.

The spacesuit's gloves contain tiny heaters in every finger.

If an astronaut must pee during a spacewalk, they wear a Maximum Absorption Garment (adult diaper).

The backpack contains the life support system, including oxygen, a cooling system and a battery.

Tethers connect the astronaut to the ISS.

Spacesuits have many layers of material to protect the astronaut, including Kevlar for strength and protection, and Mylar for insulation.

There's a lot of garbage, or "space junk," in orbit around the Earth. Space junk orbits Earth ten times faster than a bullet! Fortunately, space is big, and the International Space Station (ISS) must only occasionally avoid debris.

Flight controllers have an imaginary box around the ISS known as the "pizza box." The box is 25 kilometres to a side, and about a kilometre thick. If flight controllers predict that any space junk might enter this box, they must decide whether to dodge it.

If the ISS must avoid the debris, a Debris Avoidance Maneuver (DAM) occurs. A DAM uses **thrusters** to push the ISS into a slightly different orbit to avoid the debris.

Damage to the ISS's solar array from space junk.

The Canadian military's Sapphire surveillance **satellite** helps to track space junk.

Damage to one of the ISS's radiators from space junk.

This is the Haystack Radio Telescope in Massachusetts. It is part of a network of radar systems designed to track space junk.

Tracking Space Junk

Tracking space junk is done primarily using radar, but also using telescopes and cameras on satellites.

45 Satellite Deployment

Did you know that it costs about $100 million to launch a rocket into orbit? That's why several satellites often launch on a single rocket. If the satellites are tiny, the rocket can carry many of them! The ISS has been used to deploy many small satellites.

Small satellites arrive at the ISS as cargo. Astronauts carry the satellites to the Japanese airlock. Most of the satellites are **CubeSats**, which are deployed using the Japanese Small Satellite Orbital Deployer, or J-SSOD. This device is attached to the Japanese robotic arm.

Cyclops is a tool that deploys oddly shaped satellites. It is connected to Canadarm2. Like the Japanese system, these satellites are placed in the airlock by astronauts. Cyclops grabs the satellites from the airlock and releases them into orbit.

Cyclops

Cyclops is based on the acronym SSIKLOPS, which stands for Space Station Integrated Kinetic Launcher for Orbital Payload Systems.

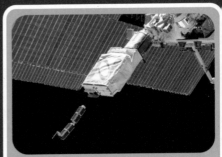

The J-SSOD attached to the Japanese robotic arm, deploying several CubeSats.

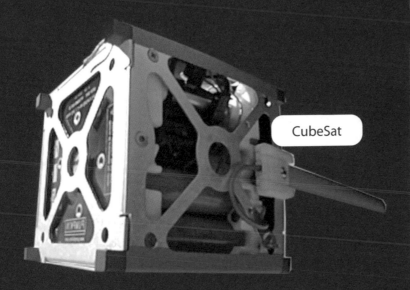

CubeSat

A satellite called SpinSat being deployed by Cyclops.

46 Special Delivery!

It takes a lot of supplies to keep International Space Station (ISS) crews healthy and happy. Astronauts on six-month missions require far more supplies than they can bring with them. That means that cargo vehicles must visit the ISS to deliver important supplies like food and experiments.

Each resupply craft holds between 3,000 and 4,000 kilograms of cargo. Astronauts eat about 1 kilogram of food each day. For 6 astronauts, that's over 2,000 kilograms per year. Astronauts also need thousands of kilograms of clothes!

Launch of a SpaceX Falcon 9 rocket on a resupply mission to the ISS.

Care Package

At the very last minute, before the cargo ship leaves Earth, a special care package including fresh fruits is added to the spacecraft.

A view inside the Cygnus cargo vessel stocked full of supplies bound for the ISS.

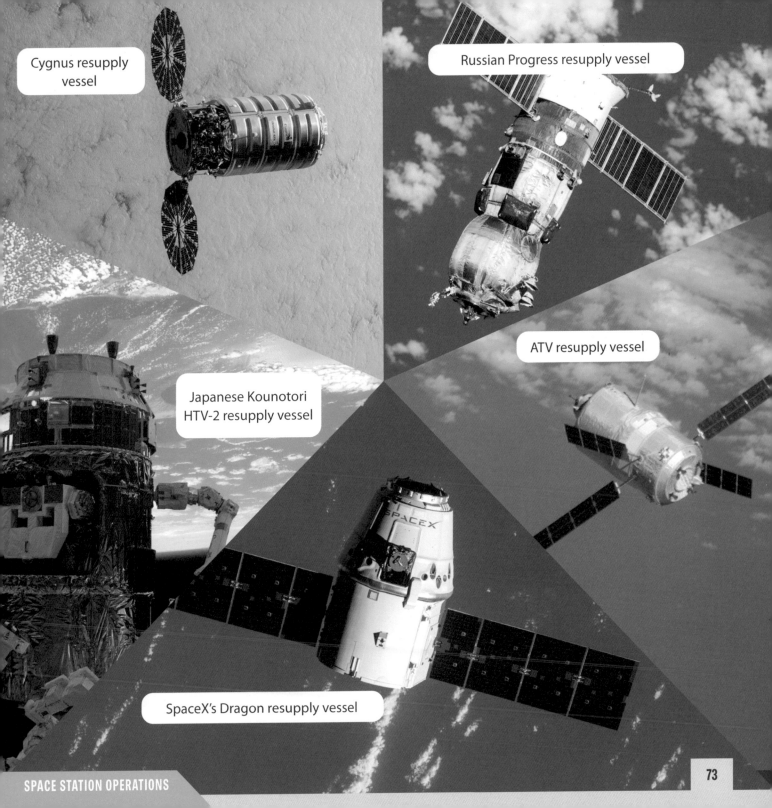

Cygnus resupply vessel

Russian Progress resupply vessel

ATV resupply vessel

Japanese Kounotori HTV-2 resupply vessel

SpaceX's Dragon resupply vessel

Astronauts do chores to keep the International Space Station (ISS) clean and safe. But what if these chores could be done by robots? The ISS is home to several robots. Some are controlled by people on Earth, and some can do their work without humans at all.

The first flying robots on the ISS were called SPHERES. This stands for Synchronized Position Hold, Engage, Reorient, Experimental Satellites. These robots use compressed gas for propulsion and a smartphone for the cameras and brain.

The latest robot assistants are called Astrobees. Each Astrobee has its own name, like Honey and Bumble. These robots push air through vents to move and use cameras for navigation.

Astronaut and flight surgeon Serena Auñón-Chancellor with two SPHERES robots. Students on Earth had programmed these flying robots to pilot themselves through an obstacle course on the ISS.

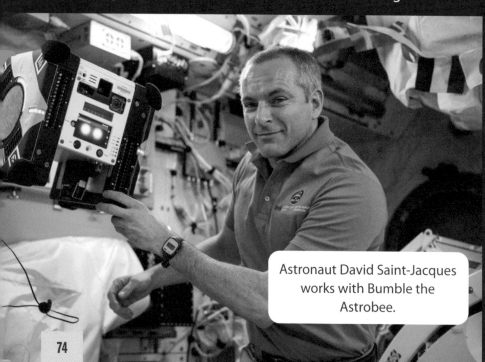

Astronaut David Saint-Jacques works with Bumble the Astrobee.

Bumble the Astrobee

48 Tourist Destination

Did you know that people have paid millions of dollars to visit the ISS? Between 2001 and 2009, seven tourists travelled to the ISS. These individuals launched aboard the Russian Soyuz spacecraft.

"Private astronauts" went through the same training as the astronauts who travelled to space in Russian rockets. This meant living in Russia, and training at Star City. Space tourists aren't just along for the ride. From launch until landing, they're given jobs aboard the Soyuz and conduct experiments on the ISS.

Dennis Tito, the first space tourist

Guy Laliberté, Canada's first space tourist, is the co-founder of Cirque du Soleil.

Anousheh Ansari was the first female space tourist. She is an Iranian American and CEO of the X Prize Foundation.

Other Space Tourists

Other spaceflight participants include Mark Shuttleworth, Richard Garriott, Gregory Olsen and Charles Simonyi.

49 Anomalies

Things go wrong every day on the International Space Station (ISS). It's usually computer glitches, stuck bolts or clogged toilets. Mission controllers, astronauts and engineers are constantly problem solving. It's all just part of the job!

When things go wrong in space, it's called an **anomaly**. Even when a rocket explodes, you may hear mission controllers say, "We've had an anomaly aboard the spacecraft."

Faulty Spacesuit

In 2013 a spacesuit malfunctioned, and water leaked into the helmet, putting an astronaut at risk of drowning.

The most serious failure to date aboard the ISS occurred on December 11, 2013. A pump in the cooling system failed, putting the ISS at risk of overheating. Everything was put on hold as engineers on Earth raced to find a solution.

Eventually the pump was replaced during two risky spacewalks totalling 13 hours. On Christmas day, the repair was completed and, with much celebration, life on the ISS went back to normal.

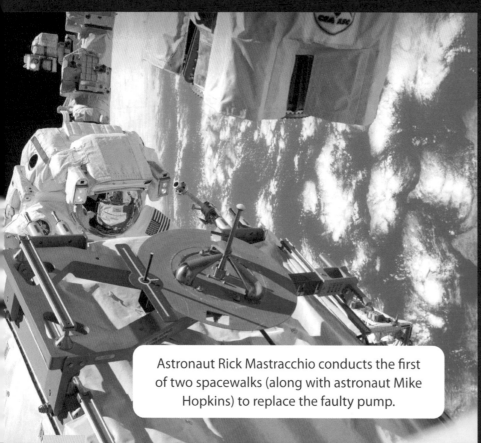

Astronaut Rick Mastracchio conducts the first of two spacewalks (along with astronaut Mike Hopkins) to replace the faulty pump.

50 Returning Home

At the end of their mission, astronauts board a spacecraft and head back to Earth. The trip home takes only a few hours, but it's far from easy.

After the spacecraft undocks, **retro rockets** change its orbit so that it meets the atmosphere. Earth's atmosphere is used to slow the spacecraft. It's a bumpy and fiery ride as the spacecraft's speed is changed to heat.

Returning to Earth is very hard on the human body, especially after six months or more in space. Astronauts may look happy when they exit the spacecraft on Earth, but they feel terrible. After a few days, they feel normal again, eager to prepare for their next mission.

Before their retirement in 2011, the space shuttles would land on a runway like an aircraft either in Florida or California.

Drop the Mic!

One of the funnier consequences of returning to Earth's gravity is that stuff doesn't float when you let go. Because of this, astronauts frequently drop things when they return to Earth.

From 2012 to 2020, astronauts returned to Earth with their cosmonaut colleagues in the Soyuz capsule. The Soyuz lands in a desert in Kazakhstan. It uses parachutes to slow its descent, and rockets at touchdown to soften the landing.

In 2020, for the first time in 45 years, the first crewed space capsule landed in the ocean. The SpaceX Dragon 2 spacecraft (named *Endeavour*) carried astronauts Robert Behnken and Douglas Hurley to the ISS and back. This mission, called Demo-2, was the first time a commercially developed spacecraft had flown to orbit with humans.

Appendix 1. Future of the ISS

The International Space Station (ISS) has a special place in our hearts. It's sad to think that someday its time will end. The ISS will operate as long as there is funding, but it's getting old. Missions will continue until at least 2028, when the ISS will be 32 years old! Can you imagine driving a 32-year-old car?

Astronauts will leave the ISS for the last time at the end of its life. They'll take all the important experiments with them. Mission controllers will use the remaining fuel and pilot the ISS into Earth's atmosphere. It will burn up over the ocean, far from any people.

Salvage

It's likely that not all of the ISS's modules will be **deorbited**. Some modules may remain in orbit as the foundation for future commercial space outposts.

From Dust to Dust

An uncrewed Cygnus cargo vessel burns up in Earth's atmosphere. When the ISS reenters, it will look something like this.

Appendix 2. Future Space Stations

The ISS wasn't the first space station, and it won't be the last! The next NASA space station is called Lunar Gateway. It is planned to be launched into the Moon's orbit in 2024.

Lunar Gateway will be located beyond Earth's magnetic field. This means that it must be adapted to a much harsher space environment. Astronauts will live and work on Lunar Gateway for much longer than the Apollo missions in the 1960s and 1970s.

This space station will be used for crewed missions to the surface of the Moon. It may even become a staging area for humanity's first crewed missions to Mars.

Lunar Gateway with Orion spacecraft docked

Appendix 3. Activities

Spot the International Space Station (ISS) from your backyard!

Did you know you can see the ISS pass overhead? When it does, it is usually the brightest thing in the night sky besides the Moon. The best time to see the ISS pass overhead is either shortly after sunset or before sunrise. At these times sunlight reflects off the ISS's solar panels, making it appear very bright. If the ISS passes in the middle of the night, you might not see it at all since it is covered by Earth's shadow.

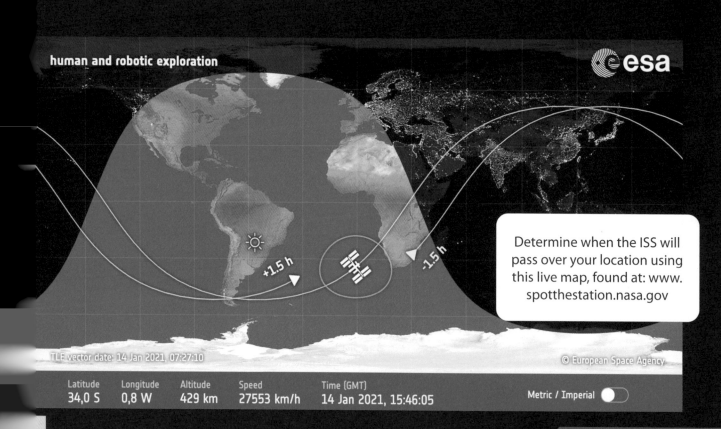

human and robotic exploration

esa

+1.5 h

-1.5 h

Determine when the ISS will pass over your location using this live map, found at: www. spotthestation.nasa.gov

TLE vector date: 14 Jan 2021, 07:27:10

© European Space Agency

Latitude	Longitude	Altitude	Speed	Time (GMT)
34,0 S	0,8 W	429 km	27553 km/h	14 Jan 2021, 15:46:05

Metric / Imperial

Photographing the ISS

Did you know you can photograph the ISS from Earth with a telescope? Many amateur astronomers have taken amazing pictures of the ISS from their own backyards! How do they do it? In most cases, they use a telescope and a digital camera. They take lots of pictures of the ISS while it passes over and pick out the best ones to share.

Newtonian telescope

Rigel QuikFind for aiming

Camera connected to the telescope using a t-adapter and a Barlow lens

Remote shutter

Image of the ISS taken by the author in 2013

You can take a photograph of the ISS without a telescope. It will appear as a dot or a streak of light depending on your camera settings. This is an iPhone photo of the ISS after sunset.

Aerosols — Particles in the air, such as dust, steam or pollution. Refers to both natural and human-made sources.

Anomaly — A problem with a spacecraft, sometimes resulting in the destruction of the vehicle.

Aquanauts — A term used to describe astronauts while training underwater, generally at the Aquarius underwater laboratory.

Berthing — The process of attaching a module or cargo spacecraft to the ISS using a robotic arm.

Bends — Sickness caused by a rapid change in air pressure.

Centripetal Force — A force felt by an object moving along a circular path.

Command Module — The part of the spacecraft from which the vehicle is controlled, like the bridge of a ship.

Cosmonaut — A Russian astronaut. Also refers to astronauts from the former Soviet Union.

CubeSat — A small satellite, typically 10 cm to a side and about 1 kg in mass.

Deorbit — The process of returning a spacecraft to Earth's atmosphere from orbit.

Docking — When a spacecraft joins with the ISS under its own power.

Experiment — Testing a hypothesis (educated guess or prediction) in a controlled manner.

Extravehicular Activity (EVA) — Also known as a spacewalk, when an astronaut or cosmonaut leaves a spacecraft in a spacesuit.

Extremophiles — Living organisms that can survive in extremely harsh environments.

Facility — A set of equipment on the ISS dedicated to a specific type of experiment or investigation.

g force (or g load) — Short for "gravitational force," it is a force like gravity that an astronaut feels while a spacecraft is accelerating or changing direction.

Gimbal — A mechanical joint that allows for rotation.

Glovebox — A box for conducting experiments accessible via pairs of rubber gloves.

Hydrolab — A pool in Russia for training cosmonauts and astronauts using an underwater mockup of the ISS.

Investigation — Simpler than an experiment, an investigation only involves collecting data, not testing a hypothesis.

JAXA — The Japanese space agency.

Low Earth Orbit — An orbit of less than 2,000 km above the Earth. This is where the space station and most satellites reside. Speeds of around 28,000 km/hour must be reached to stay in this orbit, otherwise a spacecraft will fall to Earth.

Microgravity — A term used to describe the feeling of weightlessness experienced aboard a spacecraft in orbit.

Mockup — A model of the ISS or other spacecraft used on Earth for training purposes.

Module — Pressurized habitats where astronauts live and work. There are currently 16 modules on the ISS, including the labs, nodes, and airlocks.

Node — A pressurized module to which several other modules or spacecraft can be berthed.

Operating System — Software on a computer on which other applications are run.

Orbit — The path an object (like a spacecraft) takes around a planet, moon or star.

Parabolic Flight — A path flown by a large jet aircraft to simulate weightlessness (AKA microgravity).

Remote Sensing — Using radar, lasers or imaging to make scientific observations from an orbiting spacecraft.

Retro Rockets — Rockets used to slow down a spacecraft, usually with the intention of reentering the atmosphere.

Roscosmos — The Russian Space Agency.

Russian Orbital Segment — The side of the International Space Station containing Russian modules.

Satellites — Uncrewed spacecraft in orbit of the Earth.

Spaceflight Readiness — Training involving jet aircraft, where astronauts experience high g loads and complex decision making.

Star City — A former Soviet secret city used to train cosmonauts. Currently used to train cosmonauts and astronauts on Russian hardware.

Soviet Union — The largest country in the world from 1922 to 1991. The Soviet Union divided into 15 independent countries, the largest of which is Russia.

Thrust — The force a rocket experiences while the engines are on.

Thrusters — Small rocket engines used to manoeuvre a spacecraft to change its orientation.

Telemetry — The transmission of data from a spacecraft.

Trajectory — The path taken by an object in flight.

Truss — Structure that holds together the largest components of the ISS, forming the "spine" of the space station.

US Orbital Segment — The side of the International Space Station containing the US, Canadian, Japanese and European hardware.

Parts Index

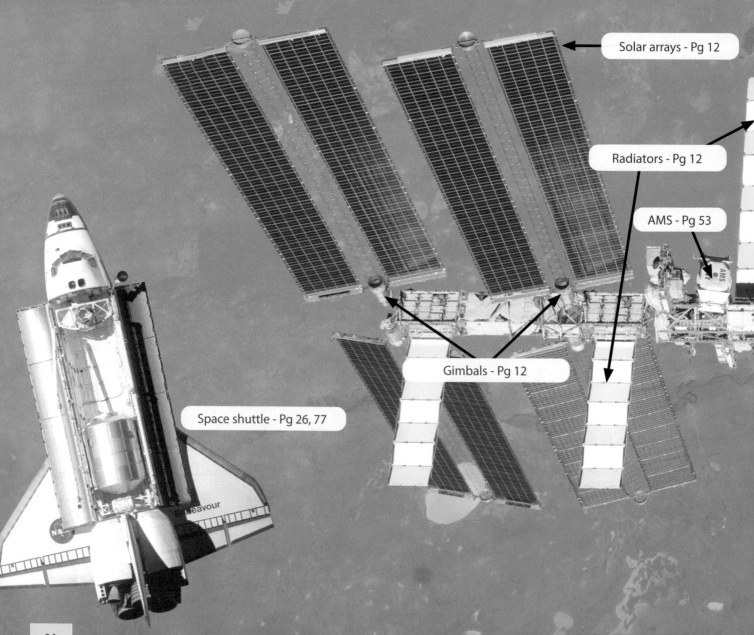

Solar arrays - Pg 12

Radiators - Pg 12

AMS - Pg 53

Gimbals - Pg 12

Space shuttle - Pg 26, 77

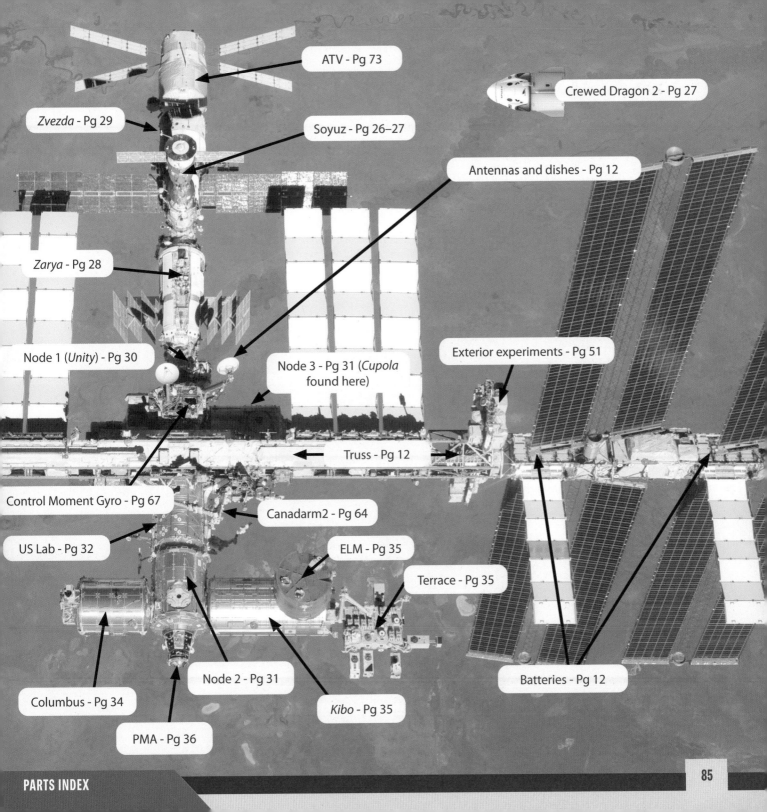

ATV - Pg 73

Crewed Dragon 2 - Pg 27

Zvezda - Pg 29

Soyuz - Pg 26–27

Antennas and dishes - Pg 12

Zarya - Pg 28

Node 1 (*Unity*) - Pg 30

Node 3 - Pg 31 (*Cupola* found here)

Exterior experiments - Pg 51

Control Moment Gyro - Pg 67

Canadarm2 - Pg 64

US Lab - Pg 32

ELM - Pg 35

Truss - Pg 12

Terrace - Pg 35

Columbus - Pg 34

Node 2 - Pg 31

Kibo - Pg 35

Batteries - Pg 12

PMA - Pg 36

The International Space Station; Operating an Outpost in the New Frontier
www.nasa.gov/sites/default/files/atoms/files/iss-operating_an_outpost-tagged.pdf

Reference Guide to the International Space Station
www.nasa.gov/sites/default/files/atoms/files/np-2015-05-022-jsc-iss-guide-2015-update-111015-508c.pdf

Research in Space 2017 and Beyond; International Space Station Facilities
www.nasa.gov/sites/default/files/atoms/files/np-2017-04-014-a-jsc_iss_utilization_brochure_2017_web_6-5-17.pdf

STEM on Station Program
www.nasa.gov/audience/foreducators/stem_on_station/index.html

Student Spaceflight Experiments Program www.ssep.ncesse.org

Summary of Scientific Breakthroughs on the ISS
www.nasa.gov/mission_pages/station/research/news/iss-20-years-20-breakthroughs

To Schedule a Classroom Chat with Astronauts on the ISS
www.nasa.gov/audience/foreducators/stem-on-station/downlinks.html

A Researcher's Guide to: Rodent Research
www.nasa.gov/sites/default/files/atoms/files/np-2015-03-016-jsc_rodent-iss-mini-book-508.pdf

The ISS Virtual Experience www.FelixandPaul.com/spaceexplorers

Live Views from the ISS www.nasa.gov/multimedia/nasatv/iss_ustream.html

Photo Credits

Adobe Stock: page 4-5, 57 (top right), 59 (center bottom, first three images and last image on far right)

Bank of Canada: page 64 (top right)

Bigelow Aerospace: page 51 (bottom right)

Chesley Bonestell: page 7

Chris Hadfield/CSA: page 45 (bottom right), 47 (top right)

Christo: page 44 (bottom right)

CMSE: page 9 (bottom right)

CSA: page 67 (top right)

Daderot: page 70 (bottom middle)

Don S. Montgomery / US Navy: page 8 (middle)

Dr. Jenni Sidey-Gibbons: page 20 (right)

ESA: page 19 (bottom), 42 (bottom left, top right), 80

Gagarin Cosmonaut Training Center: page 75 (bottom right)

Harvey Leifert: page 50 (bottom right)

JAXA: page 57 (bottom left)

John A. Read: page 81 (all)

MDA: page 70 (bottom right)

NASA: page 2-3, 4 (bottom left), 6 (top left and right), 8 (top right, bottom left), 9 (top), 10 (right), 11 (all), 12-13, 12 (bottom left), 13 (right), 15, 17 (all), 18 (all), 20 (bottom), 21 (all), 23 (top), 25 (all), 26 (all), 27 (top), 28 (all), 29 (all), 30 (all), 31 (all), 32 (all), 33 (all), 34 (all), 35 (all), 36 (all), 37 (all), 38 (all), 39 (all), 40 (top right), 41 (all), 43 (all), 44 (bottom left, top right), 45 (bottom left, top right), 46 (bottom left, bottom right), 47 (bottom left), 48, 49 (all), 51 (top right, top left, bottom left), 53, 54 (all), 55 (all), 56 (all), 58 (all), 59 (center top and second from bottom on far right), 60 (all), 61 (all), 62, 63 (all), 64 (bottom), 65 (top, bottom right, bottom), 66 (top), 67 (bottom right), 68 (all), 69, 70 (bottom left, top right), 71 (all), 72 (all), 73 (all), 74 (top right and bottom right, 75 (bottom left, top right), 76 (bottom left), 79, 84-85

NASA Analogs: page 16 (all)

NASA/Andre Kuipers: page 65 (middle)

NASA/Bill Ingalls: page 67 (top), 77 (all)

NASA/Bill Stafford: page 14

NASA/CSA: page 42 (bottom right)

NASA/David Saint-Jacques: page 74 (bottom left)

NASA/ESA/Alexander Gerst: page 78

NASA/ESA: page 40 (bottom left)

NASA/JAXA: page 22 (top right), 52 (top right)

NASA/Joel Kowsky: page 24 (bottom)

NASA/Karen Nyberg: page 76 (top right)

NASA/Lauren Harnett: page 19 (top right), 66 (bottom)

NASA/Thomas Pesquet: page 46 (top right)

Nickelodeon: page 50 (bottom left)

Penguin Random House: page 7 (top right)

Pixabay: page 52 (bottom left)

Roscosmos: page 47 (bottom right)

Spacefacts.de: page 6 (bottom left)

SpaceX: page 24 (top), 27 (right, left)

Wally Gobetz: page 22 (bottom)